T0120853

BECAUSE OF MY MOUTH

Other publications by John K. Fokwang

A Dictionary of Popular Bali Names, 3rd Edition, 2010
The Busy Spider and Other Poems, 1st Edition, 1981

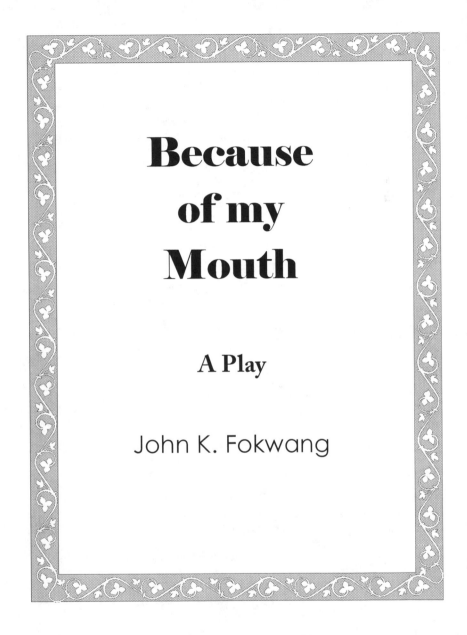

Because of my Mouth

A Play

John K. Fokwang

Spears Media Press
Denver, Colorado

Spears Media Press LLC
Denver
7830 W. Alameda Ave, Suite 103-247 Denver, CO 80226
United States of America

First Published in 2020 by Spears Media Press
www.spearsmedia.com
info@spearsmedia.com

Information on this title: www.spearsmedia.com/because-of-my-mouth
© 2020 John K. Fokwang
All rights reserved.

First Edition, 1991

No part of this publication may be reproduced, distributed, or transmitted in any form or by any means, including photocopying, recording, or other electronic or mechanical methods, without the prior written permission of the publisher, except in the case of brief quotations embodied in critical reviews and certain other non-commercial uses permitted by copyright law. For permission requests, write to the publisher, addressed "Attention: Permissions Coordinator," at the address above.

ISBN: 9781942876571 (Paperback)
Also available in Kindle (eBook)

Spears Media Press has no responsibility for the persistence or accuracy of urls for external or third-party internet websites referred to in this publication, and does not guarantee that any content on such websites is, or will remain, accurate or appropriate.

Cover art: Toh Bright; Cover design: Doh Kambem
Text design and typesetting by Spears Media Press LLC, Denver, CO

Dedicated to the youths of Cameroon.

Contents

INTRODUCTION

Because of my Mouth was originally written in 1984 and later staged in many primary schools in the North West region of Cameroon throughout the 1980s. The staged audio cassette recordings proved to be even more popular as the child actors' parents and friends replayed them at home and discussed the issues raised by the drama. The play was eventually published in 1991 for wider circulation. In this second edition, minor edits for grammar and punctuation have been made, while leaving intact, the author's voice and intent.

The play combines indigenous folklore with the predicaments posed by capitalism, urbanisation and the perceived decline in morals. It was also written during a time of growing anxiety about head-hunters who allegedly harvested the heads of unsuspecting children and adults in order to enrich themselves as quickly as possible. Such heads were believed to be in high demand in Nigeria and other European markets. The play has as its central theme, the issue of honesty and the consequences of disobeying one's parents. Originally written for and staged by children, it aimed to address these anxieties – violent crime, disobedience, parental neglect/overpampering of kids as well as the challenges posed by peer pressure.

Set in a rural community characterised by farming and trade, *Because of my Mouth* needs to be understood against the backdrop of a society experiencing rapid socioeconomic transformation. On the one hand, we see that formal western education for children is now the norm and many parents believe in its potential to transform their children's lives for the collective good. But they're also apprehensive of the supposed evils posed by the behavioural motivations of the new generation and what this would mean for their culture and legacy.

In *Because of my Mouth*, John K. Fokwang employs the format of a play to foreground and comment on critical social issues of his time. He accomplishes this by engaging both young and mature audiences as they discuss their respective concerns and challenges. In so doing, he reveals their prejudices, beliefs and shortcomings, individually and collectively. Would the issues raised in this play inspire change that could benefit both adolescents and their parents? It is our hope that contemporary readers will read and ponder on some of these issues which continue to inform our lives as they did in the 1980s.

Jude Fokwang, PhD
Associate Professor, Regis University

CHARACTERS IN THE PLAY

Nchuyekeh, main character

Sadmia, Nchuyekeh's mother

Yumbong, Sadmia's friend

Botakoe, Nchuyekeh's friend

1st Attendant

2nd Attendant

Chief

Three Nchindas

Commandant

Captain

Four Soldiers

Spectators

Notables

Any references to historical events, real people, or real locales are used fictitiously. Other names, characters, places, and incidents are the product of the author's imagination, and any resemblance to actual events or locales or persons, living or dead, is entirely coincidental.

Because of my Mouth

Act 1

ACT 1

Nchuyekeh chats with her mother who sends her to the farm. On her way she finds a head that speaks to her. She returns home and relates the incident to Sadmia.

Scene 1

As the curtain opens, Sadmia sits in a moderate parlour, knitting. She calls Nchuyekeh, who is doing her morning chores behind the house and sends her to the farm to get food for the family.

Sadmia
  Nchuyekeh! Nchuyekeh!

Nchuyekeh
  Mama!

Sadmia
  What have you been doing since morning?

Nchuyekeh
  I have been washing pans and pots.

Sadmia
  Have you washed your school uniform?

Nchuyekeh
  No mama.

Sadmia
  Don't you know [*stands up and points to her*] that today is

1

Saturday and you will go to the farm?

Nchuyekeh

I know, but I thought we're both going mama.

Sadmia

No, my daughter. We are going to cook for your uncle's send off to Kumba.

Nchuyekeh

Alright mama. I need some soap. The one I was using is finished.

Sadmia

Take one tablet of soap from the cupboard and use it carefully. [*She knits and does other things in the house*]. Nchuyekeh! Finish quickly and come. You will be late for the farm.

Nchuyekeh

I have finished mama.

Sadmia

Go to the farm at Fatu and harvest some cocoyams and plantains. Dig the cocoyams where we ended last week. Cut the small bunch of plantains I showed you.

Nchuyekeh

There are many plantains. Which is the small one?

Sadmia

The one near the big rock behind the farm hut.

Nchuyekeh

Will I be able to carry enough cocoyams and the plantains?

Sadmia

Just carry the plantain and the quantity of cocoyams that will not be too heavy for you.

Nchuyekeh

Alright mama. I'll be back soon. Keep something good for me.

Scene 2

On the way to the farm. Nchuyekeh soliloquizes as she moves to the farm. Her friends join her and they chat along the road till they part ways at the road junction to their respective farms. She continues alone and suddenly meets a head that speaks to her.

Nchuyekeh

Mothers always sit at home and send their children to far off places. Does my mother know what could happen to me today at noon tide?

Botakoe

Hello - Nchuyekeh! Are you ahead of me?

Nchuyekeh

Ah dear, I thought that I was the last one on this road to-day. What were you doing?

Botakoe

My mother increased my daily chores this morning and still asked me to go to the farm and harvest cocoyams.

Nchuyekeh

I don't know what is happening with mothers these days. They sit down and order the children to do everything in the house. Even things that they could stretch their hands and get, they would call a child from outside to come and give them such things.

Botakoe

My dear, if one does not have a ton of patience, one can't live successfully with parents these days.

Nchuyekeh

My dear, there is really no alternative. But do you know something?

Botakoe

What may it be?

Nchuyekeh

Some time ago, I was working with my mother alongside her friends. I heard them saying that when the sun is overhead, that is when the dead or people of the underworld visit the living and call some to meet them. So, if you're unfortunate to cross paths with them, they may touch you and on your return home, you'll fall ill and die suddenly.

Botakoe

Chei! Nchuyekeh. Then, we are bound to meet our end today.

Nchuyekeh

No. They also said that you can free yourself from them if at noontide, you sit down and stay quiet for some time.

Botakoe

It may be true. Many times, I have witnessed my mother and her friends seated with their hoes between their legs and no one speaks to each other. In fact, there is some dead silence and it is only broken by the most elderly woman among them.

Nchuyekeh

I wonder if that's the reason Catholics ring the church bell at noon for prayer?

Botakoe

Well, dear. I have reached the road junction where I have to leave you. Let's proceed quickly and see who will be the first to get back to this junction.

Nchuyekeh

Botakoe, you know I still have to cross that stream *[she points over the valley as she speaks]* and go over those hills before I reach our farm.

Botakoe

It doesn't matter. You are young and swift. The first person to come back should block the other's path with elephant grass and stem leaves.

Nchuyekeh

Alright. Till we meet again. *[Exits Botakoe. Nchuyekeh moves for a while and says]* I won't carry any heavy load as my mother often wants me to do. *[She sees a head and is scared.]* E-e! *[as she jumps back]*. Terrible! what is this? Someone's head? What has happened to thieves or those who trade in human heads? Well, *[she moves forward towards it]*, let me see. *[Fearfully examines it]* Eh! I'm sorry that I can't identify whose head it is. But head, why are you lying here? *[No response]*. Head, why are you lying here?

Head

I'm lying here because of my mouth.

Nchuyekeh

Unbelievable! A head has spoken to me. This might explain why I felt my hair rising. Who has cleared this place and put this talking head there? Worst things will befall me if I continue. [*She turns back*]. I must go back home and tell my mother and the chief.

Scene 3

Nchuyekeh meets her mother at home, tells her what befell her on the way to the farm and insists on going to tell the chief.

Nchuyekeh

Ma-ma, mama!

Sadmia

My dear daughter! What? Have you reached the farm and come back so soon? Or is there something wrong?

Nchuyekeh

Nn-no, mama. [*She puts her right forefinger on her lips*]. Mm-but there is something wrong. When the sun was overhead, I felt as if something would go wrong and it happened.

Sadmia

What happened, my daughter?

Nchuyekeh

Hmm... I saw a head on a clearing at the right-hand side of the road and it spoke to me.

Sadmia

What? What type of head was it?

Nchuyekeh

It was a human head and it looked fresh. I was afraid to continue my journey under the hot sun. So, I've come back to inform you.

Sadmia

Stop that nonsense! How can a head speak by itself? Where did you see it my daughter? [*she beckons her*] Come and tell me.

Nchuyekeh

Mama, [*standing quite close to her*] I saw it along the path near Mrs. Bafon's farm plot.

Sadmia

Did it speak to you immediately you saw it?

Nchuyekeh

No, mama. When I saw it, I was shocked; I picked up courage and went near to examine it.

Sadmia

Oh Nchuyekeh! Who gave you the courage to go near a head to the extent of questioning it?

Nchuyekeh

Mother, [*throwing both hands open*] did I do a bad thing? I thought it could be the head of one of our relatives.

Sadmia

No, you didn't. But what did it say?

Nchuyekeh

As I was unable to identify it, I questioned it as to why it was lying there and it replied that it was lying there because of its mouth.

Sadmia

Nchuyekeh, that was very risky. Don't do that next time.

Nchuyekeh
Why?

Sadmia
Yes, ask me why. Do you know that those who kept the head could also cut off yours if they had met you there?

Nchuyekeh
Well, mother, forgive me.

Sadmia
See, you have wasted our time today. What shall we prepare for dinner this evening?

Nchuyekeh
I'm sorry for that mama. Is it true that people really trade in human skulls?

Sadmia
So you have not heard of the incidents that took place in Bamenda, Douala, and Yaounde some time ago? Such people usually kidnap the person to a hidden place before he or she is beheaded.

Nchuyekeh
Horrible! And the government doesn't know?

Sadmia
They don't. Only after they are informed of such incidents can they act.

Nchuyekeh
If this isn't checked in those towns, this may be the beginning of it in our village. The one I saw must have been kept by those traders and they might have been searching for more.

Sadmia

You can't be too sure. Do you know the type of heads the dealers look for?

Nchuyekeh

No, mama. What shall we do?

Sadmia

Hmm... Now that your father isn't around, I don't exactly know what we should do. After all, since you have come back safely, why worry about it?

Nchuyekeh

I think that this news will please the chief and he may send his soldiers to track down the dealers. I want to go tell him.

Sadmia

Why? A small girl like you? You will not be allowed to see him. Even if you tell the palace retainers, they will not inform him. If the police or gendarmes were nearer, you could have informed them.

Nchuyekeh

I'm small but I'll try. If the palace retainers refuse, I will insist until I succeed. Given my size and age, they will realise that there is something serious in my news.

Sadmia

Nchuyekeh, don't go. I don't think you should go there. Get the remaining garri and okra and prepare dinner for us tonight.

Nchuyekeh

Mama, let me go. I'll succeed. If I finish late, then I'll go tomorrow after church.

Because of my Mouth

Act 2

ACT 2

Botakoe talks to Nchuyekeh and Yumbong to Sadmia respectively about the head incident, but Nchuyekeh insists on going to tell the chief of the village.

Scene 1

Nchuyekeh on her way to the palace. As the curtains open, Botakoe is walking on the road. Nchuyekeh calls her from behind and chats with her. She tells her what happened that day and her intentions. Botakoe advises her not to go but she insists she'll go.

Nchuyekeh

Ah Botakoe! Did you see the grass I put on your path?

Botakoe

Yes. How did you travel to that farm, harvest the crops and come back earlier than I did?

Nchuyekeh

You know I'm smart. Moreover, you told me to run and I did.

Botakoe

It's a lie. Even if you ran, I was sure to come back first. I'm convinced you got your foodstuff from a different farm.

Nchuyekeh

You are right dear. You know what?

Botakoe

I'm listening.

Nchuyekeh

Indeed, I did not reach the farm.

Botakoe

What happened?

Nchuyekeh

After you left me, I travelled only about a kilometre and found a human head lying on a clearing near Mrs. Bafon's farm.

Botakoe

Was it placed there to stop you from going to the farm?

Nchuyekeh

You look foolhardy. Why do you ask such a question?

Botakoe

I have asked because if I were you, I would have ran faster and gone to the farm and on my return, I would wait and walk with the farmers who would be returning home.

Nchuyekeh

Dear, I must confess. I don't have such a heart.

Botakoe

What did you do then?

Nchuyekeh

I moved forward and backward *[she skips in like manner]* trying to identify it but I couldn't.

Botakoe

Was that all?

Nchuyekeh

No. as I was unable to identify the head, I stood aside and asked it why it was lying there.

Botakoe

You see, you said I'm foolhardy. Can you now see that you are foolhardier than I? Instead of running away, you stood still. Did you know those who kept it there?

Nchuyekeh

No, Botakoe, I thought I was doing a good job.

Botakoe

Anyway, did the head reply to your question?

Nchuyekeh

Botakoe, my dear, the head shocked me.

Botakoe

By doing what?

Nchuyekeh

It told me it was lying there because of its mouth.

Botakoe

Ah ha! and you had what your mouth wanted.

Nchuyekeh

If you were the one, what would you have done?

Botakoe

I've told you already. But what did you do when it spoke to you?

Nchuyekeh

That's when I became afraid. I picked up my things and ran home. However, I forgot the cutlass I was going to use to harvest the plantains.

Botakoe

Are you saying that your mother does not train you to bear certain things and to oversee many things? If you were the mother in your own house and ran the home like that, what would your husband and children eat?

Nchuyekeh

What is that? Would he not send me to the daily market to get some food items there?

Botakoe

Not all husbands would do that. In your case what did your mother do?

Nchuyekeh

She blamed me and advised me to never behave as such again.

Botakoe

Where are you going now?

Nchuyekeh

I'm on my way to the palace to tell the chief.

Botakoe

Wa-La! To tell him what?

Nchuyekeh

To tell him that I saw a head and it spoke to me.

Botakoe

Nchuyekeh! You are being childish. Of what use will this be to the chief?

Nchuyekeh

Well, dear, you know how many people have begun trading in human heads. I hear one costs over a million francs. So, men with no morals behead people to sell in order to become millionaires overnight.

Botakoe

It may be true. I remember my father was telling my mother about the incident that took place in Douala. What do you think the chief will do?

Nchuyekeh

I just want to do my civic duty of informing him about what is happening in his chiefdom.

Botakoe

Yes, but one of your parents ought to go. You may get there and out of fright, be unable to speak well and get into more problems. I advise you to go back and let your mother or father deliver the information to the chief.

Nchuyekeh

Thank you, Botakoe. But I won't go back home. I must go. I will give the message correctly.

Botakoe

You know that children's reasoning faculties are not as those of adults.

Nchuyekeh

Does that matter? Children learn from adults and vice versa.

Botakoe

Alright dear, try your luck. Maybe the palace attendant will allow you to see the chief.

Nchuyekeh

That's nothing, I'll convince them. See you another day, bye.

Botakoe

Bye.

Curtain

Scene 2

Sadmia and Yumbong [A knock on the door]

As the curtain opens, Sadmia is sitting in the parlour knitting. There is a knock on the door. Yumbong enters and they chat together on current issues including Nchuyekeh's matter.

Sadmia

Come in please.

Yumbong

Good morning Sadmia.

Sadmia

Good morning Yumbong. How are you doing?

Yumbong

I'm well. Thank you.

Sadmia

What is the news from your side of the village?

Yumbong

Haven't you heard that Foncham beat his wife the other day and she was admitted in the hospital.

Sadmia

No. we, in the suburbs hardly hear current news. What happened?

Yumbong

I heard that Foncham came back from his drinking spree and asked for food. When his wife delayed in bringing it, he fell on her and beat her mercilessly.

Sadmia

It's really a curse to be married to a drunk. Men never know that alcohol brings turmoil, poverty and broken homes.

Yumbong

Most men say that drinking reduces their family problems but this is yet to be proven.

Sadmia

Those are the people who rob Paul to pay Peter. Well, that's life.

Yumbong

Sadmia, where is Nchuyekeh? I have not seen her since I came in.

Sadmia

Ah Yumbong, Nchuyekeh nearly died yesterday.

Yumbong

From what?

Sadmia

She left for Fatu to harvest some food. She says she saw a human head near Mrs. Bafon's farm and it spoke to her.

Yumbong

[*Startled*]

Don't say that. Can a human skull speak after it has been cut off from the body?

Sadmia

That is what she said, but I have not found out whether it is true from other women who went to Fatu yesterday.

Yumbong

Where is she?

Sadmia

I don't know. She insisted on going to the palace yesterday evening to tell the chief. I refused to let her go, but she was firm on going there. Whether she has stealthily left for the palace, I'm not aware.

Yumbong

Chei! the children of today! How bold was she to talk to a head and now she is bent on telling the chief. Our chief is a very stern man and if he finds out it's a lie, she will be severely punished.

Sadmia

Yumbong, you know that our days are gone. The children we have today say we only give them their bodies and they bring their hearts themselves. I did my duty by dissuading her but if she has gone there, we'll wait for the consequences.

Yumbong

Sometimes, children think they are right while their parents are wrong. This unpardonable behaviour portrayed by our young generation who will be the mothers and fathers of tomorrow gives a bad impression of how they'll manage our estates after we are gone.

Sadmia

What else can we do? You can adopt a child but a child cannot choose its mother or father.

Yumbong

It would be better to find out from some men or women who went to Fatu yesterday if they found the head and whether it was able to speak.

Sadmia

Well, I'll try to go out and ask her friends whether they have seen her since church service was over this morning.

Yumbong

Please, do. If you can't trace her, send someone or go to the palace to search for her there. I'll leave you now so that you go ahead with the search.

Sadmia

Thank you. I'll keep you informed about the matter. Bye!

Because of my Mouth

Act 3

ACT 3

Nchuyekeh goes to the palace and is bent on talking to the chief. While with the chief, she insists on the fact that the head spoke to her and soldiers take her to the head. The head refuses to talk and Nchuyekeh is beheaded and the two heads talk.

Scene 1

At the palace. It opens with two palace attendants sitting at the palace gate. Nchuyekeh meets them and introduces her mission and insists on seeing the chief herself till she is let in to talk to him.

Nchuyekeh
Good Afternoon, sir.

1st Attendant
Good afternoon my daughter. Can I help you?

Nchuyekeh
Yes, sir. I want to see the chief.

1st Attendant
What? Why do you want to see the chief? What is the important news that has brought you to the palace? Let me inform you that not everyone is allowed to talk to him.

Nchuyekeh
I know that. My message is urgent and I must be the one to tell him.

2nd Attendant

No matter how important your message may be, you should tell us to inform him. That is the tradition. He can only call you in after hearing the message from us.

1st Attendant

Only special persons go and talk to him directly.

Nchuyekeh

Sir, lead me [*points towards the inside of the palace*] to where the chief is. I have told you that I will be the one to talk to him. I want to go back quickly. If you delay me here, my message will lose its value. Please tell the chief that I have a vital message for him.

1st Attendant

[*Turns to his friend*] There may be something serious in what this young girl wants to tell the chief. Go and tell him that there is a girl here who wants to see him.

2nd Attendant

There seems to be nothing serious. Except that she may be looking for a way to marry the chief. You know there are many more women than men, so smart girls look for their husbands early enough for fear of remaining single. Anyway, let's do what she wants. [*Goes to the chief*]. Your highness, there is a very beautiful girl in the waiting room who says she brought an urgent message for you.

Chief

A beautiful girl? From where?

2nd Attendant

She is from our village.

Chief

Has she not told you the message?

2nd Attendant

No, your highness. She says that she is the only person who can tell it to you.

Chief

Whose daughter is she?

2nd Attendant

I do not know.

Chief

You foolish attendant! What is your duty at the gate? Find out and let her come in. [*To his Nchindas*] Perhaps, she could make a good wife.

Nchindas

Mbeh.

2nd Attendant

Young girl, from which quarter do you come?

Nchuyekeh

I come from the Hausa quarter.

2nd Attendant

Who is your father?

Nchuyekeh

I'm the daughter of Papa Tita.

1st Attendant

Where is he? He ought to come with you.

Nchuyekeh

He went to Limbe to see my brother who had a motor accident.

1st Attendant

Why did your mother not come with you?

Nchuyekeh

She is busy. My uncle is on a transfer to Kumba and his send-off party is today.

2nd Attendant

Alright, come with me. Squat as I'll do, clap and then tell the chief your message. [*They enter and clap according to their tradition*]. Your highness, here is the girl. She is the daughter of Papa Tita from Hausa quarter.

Chief

Good, my daughter, what is the matter?

Nchuyekeh

Your highness, I've come to tell you that traders in human heads have reached our village.

Chief

How do you know?

Nchuyekeh

I found a skull yesterday on my way to the farm and it spoke to me.

Chief

What? A skull? How was it?

Nchuyekeh

It was a human head that still had hair and flesh on it.

Chief
Where did you see it?

Nchuyekeh
I saw it on the path near Mrs. Bafon's farm plot on the road to Fatu. [*She points to the direction of the farm*]. It was lying near the road where some clearing had been done.

Chief
And you say it spoke to you. What did it say?

Nchuyekeh
When I saw it, I examined it in a bid to identify it. I asked it why it was lying there. To my greatest surprise, it replied that it was lying there because of its mouth. So I thought this would be good news for you to investigate further on those who deal with human heads.

Chief
Ha! Ha! This is incredible. Are you sure it spoke to you?

Nchuyekeh
I'm sure your highness. It really spoke to me.

Chief
I am sure that you might have heard a distant voice, and because you had asked that question it then appeared to you as if the head had spoken to you. Are you quite sure that if we go there now it will speak to us?

Nchuyekeh
Yes, your highness. That is why I came.

Chief
You are telling a lie. If a head has been cut off from the body, it is dead and thus cannot speak.

29

Nchuyekeh

There is no lie about it. This is the truth. We can go now and see. It will speak to us.

Chief

Look, little girl, if we go there and the head does not speak, I will punish you.

Nchuyekeh

Unless it's been taken away by the time we get there. Although I did not see the mouth opening, I actually heard it speak.

Chief

Fon, Ngu and Tata!

Nchindas

Mbeh!

Chief

Call for my soldiers and notables to assemble here instantly. [*after they enter and greet*]. This girl says that she found a head and it spoke to her. I have told her that a skull cannot speak and she insists that it did. Commandant, take her there and listen to what the head will say. If it does not talk to me, I will punish her.

Scene 2

Near the head. Nchuyekeh has insisted until the chief orders the soldier to take her to the place of the head. She goes there and the head does not speak. The soldiers take her and the head to chief.

Spectator

Young girl, we have come here to hear this skull speak to you. Talk to it so that we may hear it speak.

Nchuyekeh

Head, why are you lying here?

Head

Mute *[people murmur]*.

Nchuyekeh

Why are you lying here? Speak to me as you did yesterday when I passed here.

Head

Mute. *[people murmur]*

Spectator

This young girl is going to get it. She has deceived the chief and his people. She will see.

Nchuyekeh

I have not deceived the chief. It is just that I can't understand why the head cannot speak again.

Spectator

Young girl, is this the urgent message you insisted on telling the chief yourself. Let the head speak to us now.

Nchuyekeh
[*With a stick in hand*] Why are you lying here? Talk to me quickly, else I'll beat you.

Head
[*Mute*]

Commandant
Captain!

Captain
I'm at your service.

Commandant
Arrest that girl and bring her before me.

Nchuyekeh
[*crying*] Please sir, I-I kind-ly beg you to forgive me. Spare m-my life.

Commandant
My child.

Nchuyekeh
Sir!

Commandant
You have deceived the chief and his people. You insisted that you were right. His highness warned you but you did not listen. For this reason, I'll take you to him and he will punish you so that other youths may learn to speak the truth.

Nchuyekeh
Sir, I beg for your clemency. I can't understand why the head is unable to speak now. Go and tell the chief that the

head spoke.

Commandant

Handcuff this girl and let's go to the palace. Fongu get the head for the chief.

Scene 3

At the palace gate. The two attendants talk about the way youths behave these days and how Nchuyekeh was finally beheaded at the chief's instruction.

1st Attendant

Not so long ago, children were seen as innocent, playful creatures in need of special protection, and parents were fiercely determined to keep their children safe.

2nd Attendant

But today, something is decidedly different about children.

1st Attendant

Parents once felt obliged to shelter their children from life's vicissitudes, but today a great number of them operate according to new beliefs.

2nd Attendant

What is this new belief?

1st Attendant

They believe that children should be exposed early to adult experience in order to survive in an increasingly uncontrollable world.

2nd Attendant

This may be due to the fact that about two thirds of all

mothers want to work and so children are forced to become young adults and self-reliant as possible.

1st Attendant

Another reason may be the scarcity of babysitters. In the past, there were many; they were good and they stayed for a long time. Today, formal education has taken them and the few that work hard, hardly stay for long, demand high salaries and can't handle babies as those of the good old days.

2nd Attendant

I hear in some big towns a babysitter earns over forty thousand francs per month in addition to other amenities provided in the house.

1st Attendant

But while many parents urge their kids to express their feelings openly, just as they themselves were taught to do, many of them cannot conceal their distress about some of the behaviour that their attitudes seem to encourage - rudeness, whiny irritability and defiance.

2nd Attendant

Some even overpamper their children to the extent that they prefer to do the punishment meant for their children. Worst still, some create new report cards showing the children at the top of the class in order to allure interviewers and admission for them into post-primary institutions.

1st Attendant

After all, most of these parents have lots of money and under the pretext of love, they give their primary school child about 500 or 1000frs as pocket money each day.

2nd Attendant

You know what, please? I heard about a tycoon who gives

fifty thousand francs as a term's allowance to his son in
grammar school.

1st Attendant

Chei! Why would parents deceive their children that this
life is a bed of roses.

2nd Attendant

Ah ah! Haven't you heard that some of them go to confes-
sion and tell the priest that they neglected their children
because they allowed them to walk to school or failed to
give them pocket money.

1st Attendant

I know it's better to bring up one's children to respect the
authorities, to obey their parents as well as their elders and
to get used to the ups and downs of life.

2nd Attendant

It is true. But what about the children? You call them by
your side to advise them, they tell you that you delivered
them but not their hearts. They say they have the free will
to do whatever they define as right for them.

1st Attendant

Is it the result of this so-called modern civilization brought
about by western education or is it the advent of many
religious sects?

2nd Attendant

Perhaps it is the influence of other children at school or
college. In the past when children grew up with their parents, they had fewer playmates compared to our modern
school systems, so they had little or no time to imitate their
lifestyles. But today, children learn so much from their peers
during break, at play and in study groups – things that do

not advance their formal education and are generally anti-social.

1st Attendant

Should we abandon our children to teachers and the agents of modernity?

2nd Attendant

No! One must continue to bring up one's children according to the norms and mores of one's society.

1st Attendant

Even if your child disobeys you or is always impertinent you must not shun your parental responsibilities.

2nd Attendant

See this young girl who came to the palace yesterday insisting that she must see the chief. I've heard that her mother and her friend told her not to come but she insisted in doing as she wanted and came.

1st Attendant

That's how most children behave nowadays. When they reach their teens, they think they are already adults.

2nd Attendant

Why not? When they rub shoulders with adults and eat from the same dish with them, should there be any difference between them?

1st Attendant

The race is not for the swift. If you dance and exhaust yourself before the main music is played, you'd be the one to regret.

2nd Attendant

When the chief, the highest authority of this land warned this girl, she stood firm.

1st Attendant

What happened when they went to see the head?

2nd Attendant

The people who went there with her say that they saw the head still lying there but it could not speak to the girl.

1st Attendant

That's scary! What did they do then?

2nd Attendant

They said that the girl threatened the head yet it neither stirred nor said anything.

1st Attendant

What a pity! The skull which she was cocksure had spoken to her, failed her.

2nd Attendant

Of course, she was arrested by the order of the chief and taken together with the head to the palace.

1st Attendant

Do you know what the chief did?

2nd Attendant

I'm told he once again ordered the girl to make the head talk to them but she tried in vain. After a long speech in which the chief said youths today are unruly and take decisions beyond their competence; he finally meted out a heavy punishment as a deterrence.

1st Attendant

Was she sent to prison?

2nd Attendant

Which prison? He ordered his soldiers to behead her and put her head beside the one she saw. One of the notables said that a dead silence descended on the crowd as the sword fell on her and the head rolled on the ground. The bystanders shrieked and wept but were ordered to stop immediately.

1st Attendant

Hmm… The chief really did that?

2nd Attendant

You know him for his sternness and strictness. The girl pleaded for mercy but he said that other youths will learn to speak the truth and obey their parents from the example he had shown.

1st Attendant

Are we sure the youths will learn anything from such a fatal blow?

2nd Attendant

Not at all. Don't you remember the day some thieves were being executed in Bamenda and others were caught pickpocketing at the venue? While some will change, those who are set in their evil ways will continue in them. And do you know what the notable said happened?

1st Attendant

No, please tell me.

2nd Attendant

One said that when this young girl's head was put beside

the one she saw, they heard them speaking.

1st Attendant

That was very mysterious! The head that refused to talk to people then talked to another head? What did they talk about?

2nd Attendant

He said that the other head asked the girl's head why it was lying near it.

1st Attendant

What did it say then?

2nd Attendant

It replied that it was lying there because of its mouth.

1st Attendant

That was very strange! Look, the mouth makes and mars a lot of things in society. Good parents should always tell their children not to try to see everything the eyes happen to pass over or to say everything they see.

2nd Attendant

It is the opposite today. When you tell children not to do a thing, in addition to asking you why they shouldn't do it; they will secretly do it to see the consequences.

1st Attendant

Look at the youngsters who smoke banga. How many of them have gone overseas because it increased their knowledge? They only indulge in it because it enables them to become more wayward and to exploit too early what nature has in store for them.

2nd Attendant

Oh, youths of Cameroon, shall you receive the wisdom of your ancestors through your elders and parents? Or shall you create your own world with no bearing to the past?

1st Attendant

Parents, shall you leave your children to be shaped by the world or shall you continue to bring them up with morals despite the difficulties you'll encounter?

Curtains

The End.

ABOUT THE AUTHOR

John Koyela Fokwang was born in Bali Nyonga in the then British Southern Cameroons. He attended the Native Authority School in Bali where he later taught as a Probationary Teacher (1963-1965). John Fokwang continued his professional training and enrichment in 1965 and obtained his Teachers' Grade III (1968), II (1970) and Grade I in 1975. He completed his studies for the ACP in 1980 and became a Senior Grade I teacher in 1981. In the summer of 1987, John Fokwang completed studies towards a diploma in Project Management at the University of Guelph, Ontario, Canada. Always animated by the quest to enrich his professional and personal life, he trained and obtained a certificate in General Agriculture from INADES Formation Cameroon in 1998. He was a founding member of the *Association for Creative Teaching* (ACT) and the Kaberry Research Centre, Bamenda. He has edited lots of children's and teachers' literary works such as *Lion and the Monkey*. He is also the author of *A Dictionary of Popular Bali Names* (2010), currently in its third edition.

Spears Media Press LLC is an independent publisher dedicated to providing innovative publication strategies with emphasis on African/Africana stories and perspectives. As a platform for alternative voices, we prioritize the accessibility and affordability of our titles in order to ensure that relevant and often marginal voices are represented at the global marketplace of ideas. Our titles – poetry, fiction, narrative nonfiction, memoirs, reference, travel writing, African languages, and young people's literature – aim to bring African worldviews closer to diverse readers. Our titles are distributed in paperback and electronic formats globally by African Books Collective.

Visit us at www.spearsmedia.com

Printed in the United States
By Bookmasters